The editors would like to thank
BARBARA KIEFER, Ph.D.,
Charlotte S. Huck Professor of Children's Literature,
The Ohio State University, and
JIM BREHENY,
Director, Bronx Zoo,
for their assistance in the preparation of this book.

Visit us on the Web!
www.randomhouse.com/kids
www.seussville.com

Educators and librarians, for a variety of teaching tools, visit us at
www.randomhouse.com/teachers

*Library of Congress Cataloging-in-Publication Data*
Worth, Bonnie.
Would you rather be a pollywog? : all about pond life / by Bonnie Worth ; illustrated by
Aristides Ruiz and Joe Mathieu.
  p.  cm. — (The Cat in the Hat's learning library)
Includes bibliographical references and index.
ISBN 978-0-375-82883-6 (trade) — ISBN 978-0-375-92883-3 (lib. bdg.)
1. Pond animals—Juvenile literature. I. Ruiz, Aristides, ill. II. Mathieu, Joseph, ill. III. Title.
IV. Series.
QL146.3.W67 2010
591.763'8—dc22
2008033696

Printed in the United States of America   10 9 8 7 6 5 4 3      First Edition

# Would you rather be a Pollywog?

by Bonnie Worth

illustrated by Aristides Ruiz and Joe Mathieu

**The Cat in the Hat's Learning Library®**

Random House 🏠 New York

Near your house is a place
of which I am fond.
It's a body of water
that we call a pond.

I'm going to visit it.
You can come, too.
Your mother will not mind
at all if you do!

The sunshine beats down,
helping pond plants to thrive.
The plants feed pond animals
and keep them alive.

From the top to the bottom
I think that you'll see
that this pond here is lively
as lively can be!

The smallest things here
are so tiny, I hope
you've thought to bring with you
your new microscope.

Come look at this slide,
where, in one water drop,
tiny algae plants float
and animals hop.

These living things feed
a good range of creatures,
like freshwater snails and
slippery leeches.

With their teeth like files,
snails scour and glean
the algae off rocks.
They pick them quite clean!

Freshwater Snail

Algae

You might hear the buzz
of insects around.
A pond is a place
where insects abound.

"Meta-mor-pho-sis"
(which is shown on these pages)
is one great big word
for insects' life stages.

This bug changes little
from nymph to adult.
Incomplete metamorphosis
is the result.

ADULT

EGG

NYMPH

Incomplete Metamorphosis

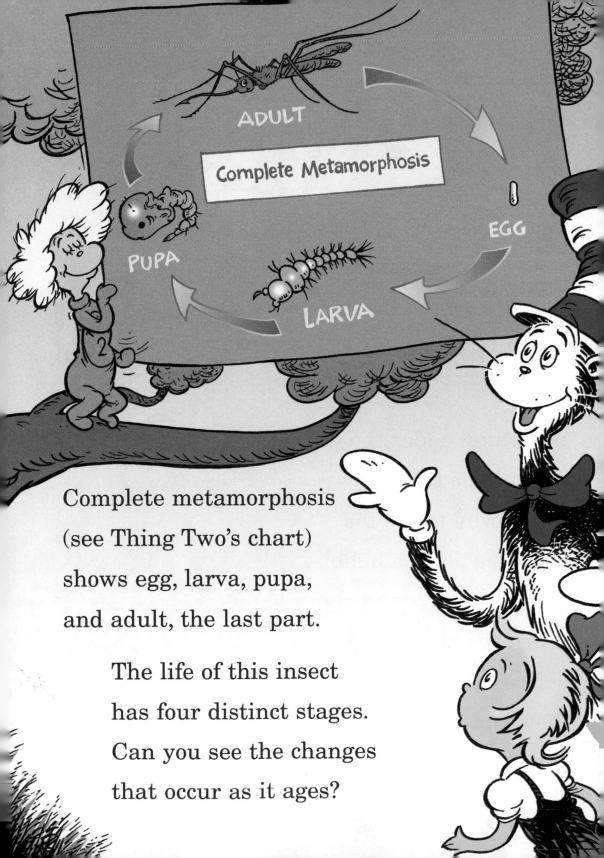

ADULT

Complete Metamorphosis

EGG

PUPA

LARVA

Complete metamorphosis
(see Thing Two's chart)
shows egg, larva, pupa,
and adult, the last part.

The life of this insect
has four distinct stages.
Can you see the changes
that occur as it ages?

Most pond insects bite.
Water boatmen do not.
As nymphs they live down
in the leaves and the rot.

Breathing under the water
is really no trouble.
They swim to the top
and drag down a bubble.

When the air is used up,
before they can drown,
they capture another
and take it back down.

When they are ready
to take off and fly,
they swim to the surface
and let their wings dry.

This is a fact
that will shock and amaze:
some insects live
only two or three days!

Before we leave insects,
let's visit one more.
It's called water strider.
In fact, I see four!

With long legs, it runs
on the water, and yet
it doesn't fall in
and it doesn't get wet.

Its belly is waterproof.
Two middle legs row.
Two hind legs steer,
you'll be happy to know.

These insects are prey
to the fish, frogs, and birds.
Of these we'll go on now
and say a few words.

SUNFISH

The sunfish can swim
near the surface, like so.
The bullhead and darter
both swim down below.

BULLHEAD

DARTER

Pumpkinseed teeth
are so sharp, they don't fail
to crush shells and eat up
the freshwater snail.

PUMPKINSEED

SNAIL

BLUEGILL

ALGAE

Bluegill eat larvae—
a fine fishy treat.
For crappie the algae
are tasty to eat.

LARVAE

CRAPPIE

These fish should be wary.
You want to know why?
Kingfisher is watching
from that tree nearby.

When the moment is right—
and this is my hunch—
it will swoop down and have . . .

. . . some fresh fish for lunch!

These ducks like to nest
in the cattails onshore,
laying three or four eggs,
and sometimes even more.

When ducklings hatch out,
they follow the mother
all in a neat line,
one after the other.

Ducklings are covered
with soft, fuzzy down.
Down helps them to float
so that they won't drown.

Mom teaches dabbling,
dunking head over feet
to fill up the bill
with good food to eat.

The grooves in their bills
drain the water, you see.
The name for the grooves?
Why, they're called "lamellae"! (luh-MEL-ee)

Lamellae

At the pond, you will meet,
if you have any luck,
a swan or a goose
or a whistling duck.

With swans or geese—
get ready for this—
their voice may come out
sounding more like a hiss.

What is that sitting over
on that fallen log?
I think you can tell me.
Of course! It's a frog.

A frog lays her eggs in
a clump, and that way
the eggs seem too big
to be eaten as prey.

EGGS

Inside of the eggs,
the tadpoles grow
the gills to breathe under
the water, you know.

In two weeks, more or less,
out pop pollywogs!
("Tadpoles" is the other
name for baby frogs.)

They try to blend in.
Look under those logs
and I think you will find
at least six pollywogs.

At five weeks, a pollywog
changes some more.
Hind legs pop out where
there were none before.

Then forelegs sprout out
from two lumps by its head.
It loses its gills
and it gets lungs instead.

Its mouth and jaw widen.
Its tail starts to shrink.

This pollywog looks
like a frog now, I think!

You may wonder what makes
that loud croaking bellow.
"Bullfrog" is the name of
the loud croaking fellow.

It puffs up and lets loose.
It's the way bullfrogs say:
"Don't try to eat me!
I'm too big! Stay away!"

You'll also find here
something else rather cute.
It's the amphibian
that's known as the newt.

NEWT

An amphibian,
just so you understand,
lives part-time in water
and part-time on land.

The newt hides its eggs
among the pond's weeds.
Weeds offer protection
a little egg needs.

EGG

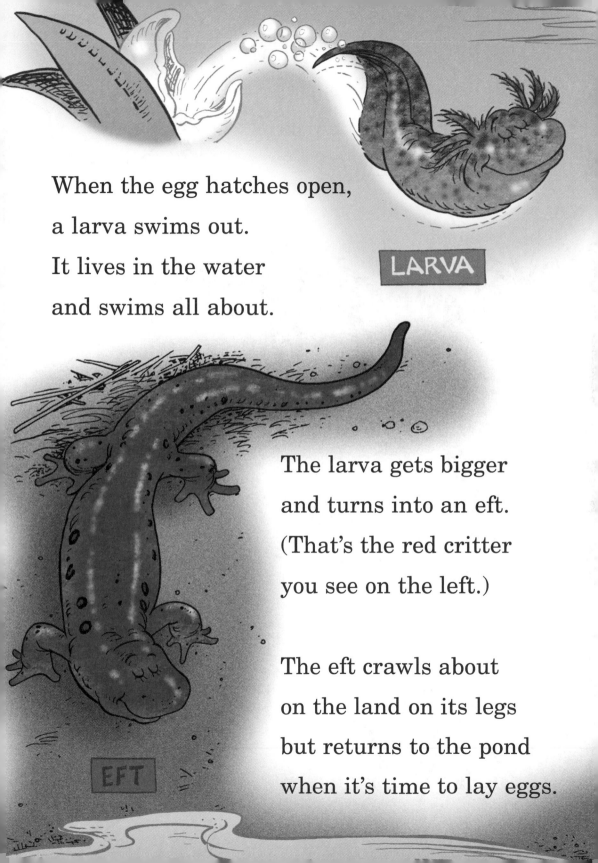

When the egg hatches open,
a larva swims out.
It lives in the water
and swims all about.

LARVA

The larva gets bigger
and turns into an eft.
(That's the red critter
you see on the left.)

The eft crawls about
on the land on its legs
but returns to the pond
when it's time to lay eggs.

EFT

Turtle buries her eggs
on the banks in the spring.
Eating bugs from the pond
is her favorite thing.

Most turtles bask
in the heat of the sun.
If you look on the rocks,
I think you'll see one.

Your mother is calling.

It's lunchtime, I see.

Tell me, which kind of pond life

would you rather be?

Of all that I've shown you—
snail, duck, fish, or frog—
I'll tell you right now that
I'd rather be a . . .

. . . pollywog!

# GLOSSARY

**Amoeba:** A blob-like organism not visible without a microscope.

**Gills:** The breathing organs of some underwater animals.

**Glean:** To gather or collect.

**Grooves:** Long, narrow cuts.

**Larva:** A young animal that changes shape (form) as it grows to become an adult.

**Microscope:** An instrument used to view things too small to be seen by the eye alone.

**Prey:** An animal hunted for food.

**Scour:** To clean by rubbing very hard.

**Spirulina:** An algae plant that cannot be seen without a microscope.

# FOR FURTHER READING

*Big Book of Bugs* by Theresa Greenaway (DK Children, *Big Books*). Get a close-up view of bugs! For grades 1–3.

*Ducks Don't Get Wet* by Augusta Goldin, illustrated by Helen K. Davie (HarperTrophy). Learn how ducks keep dry. For grades 1–3.

*From Tadpole to Frog* by Wendy Pfeffer, illustrated by Holly Keller (HarperTrophy, *Let's-Read-and-Find-Out Science*, Stage 1). An introduction to the life cycle of frogs. For grades 1–3.

*Pond Life* by Barbara Taylor (DK Children, *Look Closer*). Stunning photography of pond life. For grades 3 and up.

*What's in the Pond?* by Anne Hunter (Houghton Mifflin, *Hidden Life*). Descriptions of a variety of pond animals, accompanied by colorful illustrations. For preschool to grade 2.

*What's It Like to Be a Fish?* by Wendy Pfeffer, illustrated by Holly Keller (HarperTrophy, *Let's-Read-and-Find-Out Science*, Stage 1). Learn all about fish by studying a goldfish. For grades 1–3.

# INDEX

algae, 8, 10, 19
amoebas, 9
amphibians, 34

birds, 17, 19–25
bluegills, 19
bullheads, 18

crappies, 19

darters, 18
ducks, 22–23, 24, 39

efts, 35
eggs, 12–13, 22, 27,
    34–35, 36

fish, 17, 18–21, 39
frogs, 17, 26–32, 39

geese, 24–25

insects, 12–17, 36

kingfishers, 19–21

lamellae, 23
larvae, 13, 19, 35
leeches, 10–11

metamorphosis, 12–13

newts, 34–35
nymphs, 12, 14

pollywogs, 27–31, 40
pumpkinseeds, 18
pupae, 13

snails, 10, 18, 39
spirulina, 9
sunfish, 18
swans, 24–25

tadpoles, 27–31, 40
turtles, 36–37

water boatmen, 14–15
water striders, 16–17
worms, 11

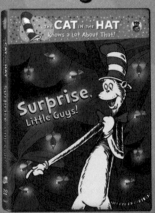